The Cosmic Quill

words that transcend the stars

Ramya Vasisht

BookLeaf Publishing

India | USA | UK

Presentation by *BookLeaf Publishing*

Web: www.bookleafpub.com

E-mail: info@bookleafpub.com

ISBN: 9789363312708

First edition 2024

To the loved ones who have been my constant source of inspiration and support.

My mother, whose unwavering love and guidance have shaped me into the person I am today.

My beloved Simba, whose unconditional love and companionship have brought joy and comfort to my life.

To those who have helped me grow and thrive in my professional journey whose leadership has been a beacon of light in my career.

To all my friends, who have been my rock, my confidants, and my partners in crime.

And to my loving hubby who has been my favourite human, my sounding board, and my forever home.

This book is a testament to the power of love and connection. Hope you find inspiration in the beauty and chaos of life!

With all my love and gratitude,

Ramya

ACKNOWLEDGEMENT

"to nature, love, life and chaos, thanks for making me who I am today."

PREFACE

This journey began with a single star, a single word. A spark of inspiration that ignited a constellation of thoughts, emotions, and reflections. As I wandered through the inner cosmos, I found myself navigating the depths of the human experience—love, loss, hope, and transformation. In the silence of the night sky, I heard the whispers of my soul. In the light of the stars, I saw the beauty of the human condition. And with each word, a poem was born—a celestial map of my inner journey. 'The Cosmic Quill' is a collection of those words, those poems, and those moments of cosmic connection. It is an invitation to join me on this journey, to explore the infinite possibilities of the human heart, and to find your own place in the vast expanse of the universe. So, let us embark on this poetic odyssey, with the stars as our guide and the words as our wings.

Cosmos

I'm tied to you—not by strings and rope
but by swerve hope…like:
The tides to moon,
A wish to boon,
Each night to stars,
The pain behind scars.

A praise to flatter
Mostly, in the physics of everything—
Like the Energy
And Matter!

In the pull of the tides, we sway,
Hope binds us like stars to the night.
A wish, a prayer, a subtle delight,
Bridges hearts, come what may.

Scars we bear, stories of past,
Echoes of pain, yet love shall last.
In the fabric of time, we find our place,
Bound by hope's grace, in cosmic embrace.

So here we stand, tethered by fate,
In the dance of existence, both small and great.
United not by mere threads of earth,
But by the eternal bond of our shared rebirth.

Finding bliss

Look out for me in the morning daylight,
As rays scatter beyond the horizon.
Listen to me in the songs of nature,
Feel me when the wind breezes out.
    I'm in the words your mind hums,
    As the first cuppa kisses your lips.
    In the bookmarked pages you reread,
    In the fragrance of pink jasmine's bloom.
    In the dewdrops of rain, so delicate,
    In the feeling as waves touch your feet by the
sea.
    In the twinkle of stars above,
    In the silent wee hours of the night.
I'm in those blissful moments,
that life breathes out, so pure and bright.

Emptiness

I miss your smile, so bright and wide,
The tiny fights, that we'd always hide,
Morning coffees, sipped side by side,
Soaking sunshine, our love's sweet pride.

From dawn to dusk, every single hour,
My heart beats for you, with every second's
power,
Each minute ticks, a longing true,
Every breath I take, thinks only of you.

In your absence, time stands still,
My days are empty, my nights grow chill,
The world moves on, but I remain,
Frozen in memories, of our love's sweet refrain.

Your smile, a ray of pure delight,
Our tiny fights, a love so strong and bright,
Morning coffees, a ritual so sweet,
Soaking sunshine, our love's retreat.

Oh, how I yearn, for your loving embrace,
To feel your warmth, in every single place,
My heart aches, with every passing day,
Until we meet, in our own sweet way.

Unreal Goodbyes

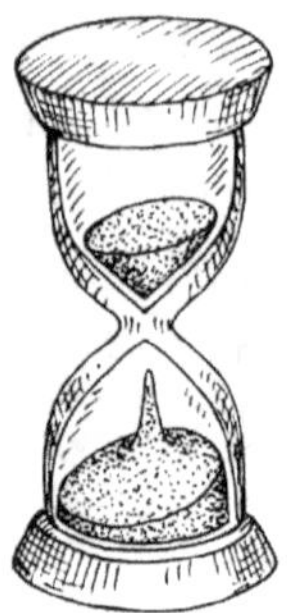

I wish you were here, near or far,
Somewhere I could reach, to hold you in my
arms.
I wish I knew the place, the time, the flight,
To hug you tight and say how grateful I am for
your light.

One chance to say goodbye, that's all I ask,
To pause time, just a minute, to kiss your hand.
But fate has taken you away, without a trace,
Leaving me with memories, a longing embrace.

Oh, how I envy those who got to say bye,
To hold their loved ones close, before they said
goodbye.
But for me, all I can do is have faith and dream,
Of meeting you again, in some lifetime's
scheme.

It's hard and sad, this longing in my heart,
But I survive on memories, our love's sweet
start.
Thank you for the time we had, the love we
shared,
In my dreams, I'll hold you close, until we meet
again, my love.

Espere Por Favor

No matter how much I ponder, some questions have only one answer—

"WAIT"

For life to reveal the mystery; unveil the glory, and unfold the story—untold!

Love is nubivagant!

Love is like a wandering cloud,
Beautifully spread all around,
Amidst silence or in a crowd,
Tranquil within and pondering loud.

Love is like clouds, closer with no bound,
Showing the way for thunder's surround;
Caught in the lightning, astound,
Seizing droplets of drizzle,
To rain over the earthy mound.

Love is like a stormy sound,
Airy, yet a feeling profound!

Heart-Sigh!

Dream big,
Let your spirit soar high,
Like kites painting the sky.
Sparkle your dreams with colours,
Give wings to your zeal,
Try without fear.

Beat the odds, forge your way forward,
Aim higher, don't fetter.
Count the minutes in making
Hours to better.

Dream big,
Let your spirit soar high.
Be an achiever,
And let your heart sigh!

A hut by the sea..

I Love the enchanting palaces and the dazzling
city lights.
The night that never ends until the daylight...and
I do love the haute couture with stylish
carry-outs.
Party places and never-ending night outs.

However, the soul seeks different
ME
My heart craves and
beats for the rhythm of a sea…
the smell of fresh air...
A walk on the shores...
While the sun is setting free in
moonlight spree…
Soul calls for a shack by the sea to BE!

You are my home...

My love for you is like the moon to earth,
A constant presence, a gentle birth.
Like a star that shines bright in the night,
You light up my life, and make everything right.

You are the sun to my sky, so warm and true,
A radiant beam that shines just for me and you.
Like a tree that roots deep into the earth,
Our love is strong, and forever of worth.

Just as the sea meets the shore, so calm and free,
My heart meets yours, in perfect harmony.
Like a fish that swims in the ocean's embrace,
I find my home, in the warmth of your loving
space.

Breathing is life, and you are my air,
Without you, I'd suffocate, and be unable to bear.
Like the soul that animates the body's frame,
You bring me to life, and make my heart
proclaim:

I love you more with every passing day,
In every way, in every moment, every way.

Rehash!

In chaos, I've lost myself, it's true,
Searching for truth, but finding only sorrow
anew.
Since you left, I've been alone, adrift,
Wondering if my heart still beats, or if I'm just a
ghostly rift.

I keep you alive in my thoughts, day and night,
My mind races, my eyes never shut tight.
Though my body sleeps, my soul remains
awake,
Longing to find you, to see your face, to hear
your gentle sake.

Happiness once had a face, and that face was
yours,
Now it's lost, and I'm left with only tears and
endless roars.
I need to find myself, to reclaim my heart,
To pull myself back from the grave, to restart.

For I'm living like a plastic flower, fake and
bright,
Never withering, never dying, but never truly
alive in sight.
My soul is numb, my heart is cold, my eyes are
dry,
But deep inside, a spark remains, a flame that
refuses to die.

Oh, how I yearn to rediscover myself, to be
whole once more,
To find my way out of this darkness, to walk
through the door.
To leave this emptiness behind, to feel the sun's
warm rays,
To love you again, to live again, to find my way
back to life's sweet ways.

Hopelessly hopeful!

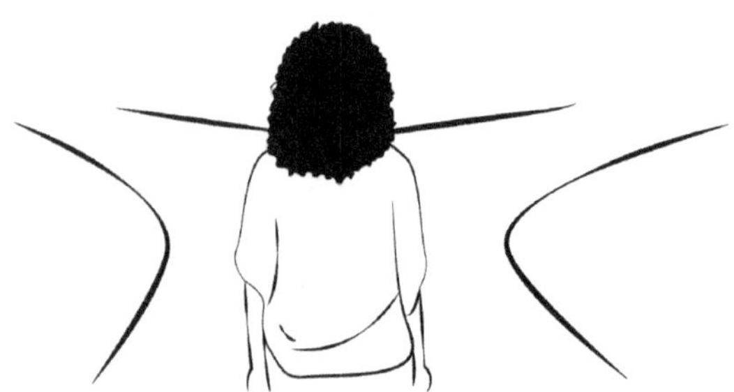

In the darkness of life's raging storm,
I stand alone, silent and forlorn,
Like a traveller lost in a forest deep,
Blindfolded, with no path to keep.

No direction to follow, no guiding light,
I wander, searching through the endless night,
Hoping for rescue, a beacon to appear,
But none comes near, and I'm left to fear.

The journey's long, the destination unknown,
I trek on, weary, with a heart of stone,
The weight of the world upon my chest,
A void that aches, a pain that finds no rest.

Like thunder, facts strike with a mighty sound,
Shaking the ground, leaving me breathless,
worn,

Draining my strength, leaving me weak and
small,
A hurt that pierces to the core of all.

Yet still I walk, through the stormy night,
For in the darkness, a spark of hope takes flight.

Invisible wings

Stay strong, dear heart, and fear not the
unknown,
For in the darkness, a light will soon be shown.
Have faith in the future, and the plans yet to
unfold,
Wait for the clouds to clear, and the sun's
warmth to enfold.

Hold on to hope, dear one, and don't let go,
For in the depths of the tunnel, a lighthouse
glows.
It guides you towards evolution, towards growth
and renewal,
So build your wings, dear heart, and prepare for
life's reveal.

Though the path ahead may seem uncertain and
long,
Know that you'll emerge stronger, with a spirit
that's strong.
So hang on to hope, and don't lose your way,
For the light at the end of the tunnel will guide
you through the day.

And when the time is right, you'll spread your
wings and fly,
Soaring high, with a heart full of joy, and a spirit
that's free to try.

Keep shining, dear heart, and never lose your
light,
For you are a beacon of hope, in the dark of
night.

Paw-some pur'fection

Tiny paws, so soft and light,
Bring healing comfort to my sight.
Innocent eyes, a precious face,
My heart beats for you, my little grace.

You're more than just a pet, a true friend indeed,
A piece of my heart, a love that's freed.
I'm grateful for your presence in my life,
A blessing from above, a love so rife.

Your purrs, a balm to my soul,
A healing touch, that makes me whole.
I wonder what life would be, without your gentle care,
But with you by my side, I know we'll face life's challenges with flair.

You have a special place, in my life's journey so far,
A constant companion, a love that's rare.
Thank you, dear cat, for being my shining star,
Forever in my heart, you'll be, near and far.

Monsoon Mood

As monsoon clouds cover the sky,
I sit with coffee, lost in thought, and sigh.
Raindrops fall like tears, a gentle hue,
Reminding me of you, and the love we once
knew.

The earthy scent of rain-soaked soil fills the air,
A fragrance that transports me to moments we
shared with care.
I wonder where you are, in this rainy spell,
And smile, thinking of the memories we've
swell.

The wind whispers secrets, as I gaze at the grey
My heart feels grateful, for the love that's still in
play.
Though we're apart, your presence is felt,
A reminder of joy, that our love has dealt.

In this cosy evening, I cherish the past,
And look forward to the future, with love that
will forever last.

Treasured Friendship

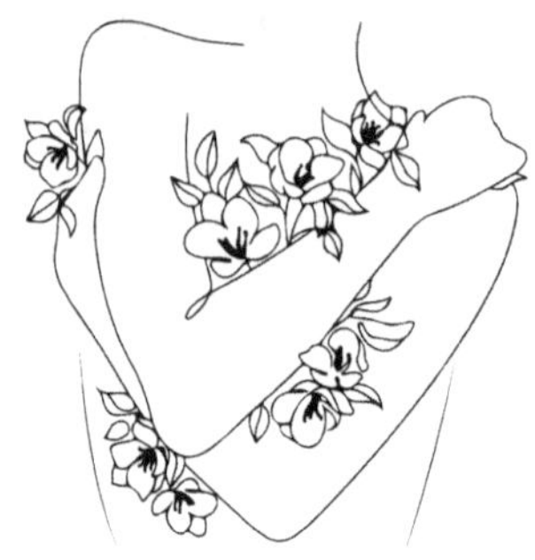

Friends like you are a precious find,
A treasure trove of love and peace of mind.
Your presence alone can calm the storm,
A soothing balm that keeps my heart warm.

Like an unwithering flower, your love shines bright,
A constant source of light in life's plight.
You shower me with positivity, with every passing day,
A reminder that friends are a gift in every way.

They say blood ties are strong, but friendship is eternal,
A bond that transcends words, a love that's unexplainable.
You are my rock, my confidant, my guiding star,
A source of strength that helps me journey far.

So here's to our friendship, a treasure so rare,
A bond that I cherish, with love and care
Thank you for being a friend, a shining light in
my life,
The unconditional bond that cuts through strife.

Resilient heart

Dear heart, don't be disappointed,
When the world pulls you down, and your
dreams are shattered.
Dear mind, don't be discouraged,
By the words and opinions that others have
scattered.

Life is to live in the present,
Not in the past, nor in the future's tension.
The brain toggles between what's been and
what's to come,
But it's in the moments that last, where love is
won.

So fuel your courage with hope and aspiration,
And aim to be a little ahead of yesterday's
worries and strife.
Dear heart, worry not, for life is too short,
To let fears and doubts dictate your every
thought.

Embrace the present, with all its might,
And shine your light, in the darkness of night.
For today is all you have, to labour with passion,
And make the most of every moment, with love
and compassion.

Sunspiration

As morning breaks, and sunbeams play,
My heart awakens, in a brand new way.
The sun's warm touch, ignites my soul,
Filling me with purpose, making me whole.

With every ray, my dreams take flight,
In the sun's embrace, all seems right.
Its light dispels doubts, and fears subside,
As sunspiration guides me, with a gentle, loving
pride.

So let us bask in the sun's glorious grace,
And let our spirits soar, in its radiant space.
For in its brilliance, we find our way,
And sunspiration lights up, a brighter day!

Morning Rays of hope

The sun blazes to shine, a fiery splendour in the
sky,
Nothing in life is easy, but its beauty makes our
spirits fly.
With every rise, it paints a new canvas, a
masterpiece so grand,
A daily reminder to chase our dreams, to reach
for the divine hand.

Its rays illuminate the path, guiding us through
life's plight,
Warming our hearts, and lighting the way,
banishing the dark of night.
Though we may think it sets, it's just an illusion,
a trick of the sight,
For the sun's true essence remains, a constant,
shining light.

Oh, majestic sun, you are the ultimate power, a
treasure so rare,
Your value is immeasurable, a gift beyond
compare.
I'm grateful for your warmth, which chases away
my fears,
Without you, I'd be lost, a shadow of my former
self, through all my tears.

Thank you for illuminating the world, for being
my guiding star,
You are my favourite thing, my daily source of
joy, near and far.
Keep shining, dear sun, and shattering the night's
disguise,
For in your radiance, we find life, and all its
beauty, opened wide, with open eyes.

Amor momma!

A mother's heart, so pure and serene,
Flows like a river, ever calm and clean.
It navigates through life's rocky flaws,
Embracing all, with a love that never pauses.

With gentle guidance, she supports our way,
Through steep and shallow waters, come what
may.
Her patience is an ocean, deep and wide,
A refuge from life's storms, where we can
reside.

Unlike nature's fury, which sometimes
unleashes,
A mother's love remains constant, never
represses.
She holds the tsunami of emotions within,
Yet stays peaceful, blessing us with love and
grace to win.

Her heart is a sanctuary, where we find solace,
A love that's infinite, forever and beyond.
A mother's heart, a treasure to behold,
A precious gift, worth more than gold.

You are my sky

In search of you, I discovered me,
A journey within, where love and light
converged to set me free.
You guided me to confront my deepest flaws,
And helped me transform, with a heart that now
pauses.

With your gentle nudge, my mind expanded its
view,
Embracing new horizons, a 360-degree
breakthrough.
I shudder to think what I'd do without your
grace,
Lost in a nomad city, a wanderer without a trace.

You're a rare gem, with thoughts as clear as day,
Genuine and heartfelt, you've shown me the
way.
You've helped me become a better version of
myself,
A treasure I cherish, a heart that's found its
wealth.

Oh, how I wish we could spend more moments
together,
Sculpting our lives, growing older, our bond will
weather.
Through life's ups and downs, I'm grateful for
your love,
A constant presence, a heart that sends me from
above.

The lipstick effect!

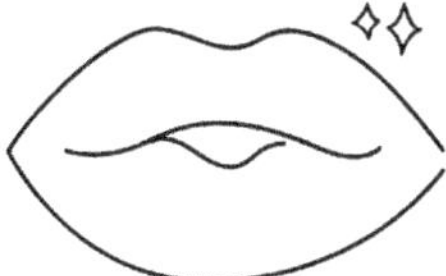

I live for lipstick, my heart's desire,
A tiny tube that sets my soul on fire.
It's more than just colour, a powerful might,
Unleashing confidence, banishing the night.

With every stroke, my spirit takes flight,
A declaration of self-love, shining so bright.
It's a symbol of strength, a beacon of grace,
A pop of colour that illuminates my face.

Lipstick is my armour, my shield and my sword,
A tool that empowers me, making me
unstoppable and bold.
It's a reminder that I'm fierce and fearless too,
A beauty that's more than skin-deep, forever
shining through.

"You on My Mind"

I close my eyes to find you,
By my side, in imagination's gentle hold.
We're together, hands entwined,
Conversations flowing, minds synchronised.
No topic needed, just random thoughts,
Arguing over movies, defending favourite
characters we've bought.
Critiquing things that don't matter, yet precious
in our eyes,
Silly moments, treasured memories that never
die.
I imagine you all the time,
Wondering if you're near, in spirit, you're
always on my mind.
Though distance separates, my heart feels you
near,
A love so strong, it transcends space and
lightyears

Your presence whispers comfort, a soothing
melody,
A bond so deep, it echoes wild and free.
In dreams, in thoughts, in every waking hour,
You're with me, a love that's always in power.

At La Plume

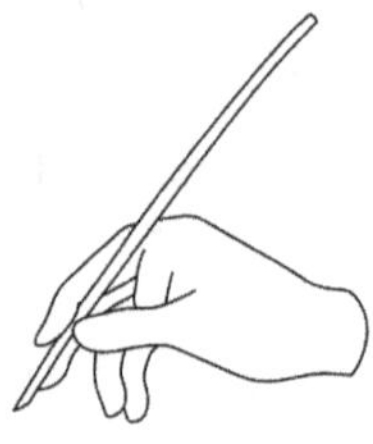

I once wondered why the pencil comes with an
eraser,
Now I understand the profound truth it brings.
It's a reminder to write without fear or
hesitation,
To let our thoughts flow, and our stories unfold
with creation.
Sometimes we write things we didn't mean to
say,
Call it mistakes, but they're just part of the way.
Use the magic of the eraser, rewrite again and
again,
For it's not what's written that matters, nor
what's erased in vain.

What matters is the intention, to etch life with
love,
To write our own story, sent from above.
Go on, write and rewrite, for you hold the
power,
To shape your destiny, each and every hour.

You may not be right always, but you have the
eraser's might,
To start anew, to etch your life, and make it
shine so bright.
Make mistakes, learn from them, and start again
with glee,
For life is to be loved, not hated, and lived wild
and free.
So write your own fate, with every line and
every word,
And remember, the eraser is there to help you be
heard.
Life is a canvas, waiting for your brushstrokes
bold,
Fill it with love, laughter, and stories yet untold.

Brewing Romance

Coffee, the spark that ignites my soul,
A flavorful love that makes my heart whole.
With every sip, my senses come alive,
Mornings are stronger, with coffee by my side.
As night descends, a rich cup is my delight,
Coffee, my eternal companion, shining bright.
If it were a person, I'd be swept off my feet,
Dark and strong, a love that none can beat.
Who wouldn't crave such a passionate affair?
A constant companion, always beyond compare.
In every cup, a smile, in every sip, a thrill,
Coffee, my heart beats for you, my love that's
real.

The Cosmic Gift

One thought sparks speculation,
One hour ignites inspiration,
One month fuels determination,
One year solidifies dedication,
One decade shapes preparation,
Until a lifetime's dream takes flight,
In my first book of poems, a heartfelt delight.
A celestial blessing from the stars above,
Reaches earth, and touches my heart with love,
It's not just passion, but a dream come true,
A testament to the power of dreams anew.

Virgo heart

I don't want life as a bed of roses,
Invisible thorns pierce, and creative souls
propose
A life of Monday's determination, not always
Sunday's rest
For in the grind, my heart finds its cosmic nest
As a Virgo's heart beats strong and true,
I crave the facts, the truth, and all that's new
No sugarcoated lies, just practical, earthy ground
My cosmic quill writes truths, with precision
unbound
Comfort's complacency makes me lazy and
blind
I'd rather face my fears, and let my analytical
mind unwind

The truth my heart tells me, though it's hard to
see
Is the beauty of imperfection, wild and carefree

I don't need wings to fly, I'm earthbound and
strong
A child of the cosmos, where my heart belongs
I'll take the truth, the struggles, and the fall
For in the darkness, my creative spirit stands
tall.

Creative crime

As I lie in bed, gazing at the ceiling above,
Scattered thoughts converge, like stars in a
cosmic love.
Where did they hide, all these days gone by?
I wonder, as I close my eyes, and let my fingers
fly.
Fresh ideas simmer, like a pot left unattended,
As I type, my brain critiques, my heart is
amended.
'Dear love, it's your life, your words, do as you
please,'
My heart whispers, and I choose to release.
With every word, a conspiracy of the conscious
mind,
Inspired by the cosmos, my soul entwines.

I pen down every thought, every phrase, every
rhyme,
Embracing the beauty of this creative crime.

City Illuminati

Heaven on earth, a city divine,
Varanasi's silken threads, Ganges' sacred shrine.
Older than tradition, history's timeless tale,
Kashi, a city of wonder, where souls set sail.

Wind whispers Vibhuti, conch shells serenade
the air,
Candlelit ghats reflect starlight, heaven's beauty
shared.
I witness spiritual reality's grand display,
Shiva, the ultimate almighty, in every heartbeat's
sway.
The city pulsates with life, yet ghats stand calm
and deep,

Ganga's rush signifies balance, in eternal sleep.
Boats navigate rushing waters, a lesson to behold,
To see eternal reality, Shiva, where death's stories unfold.
I saw pyre-lit bodies, realised our actions' temporary sway,
A fleeting life, a moment's breath, and we're away.
People seek pious death, leaving behind cherished fare,
Vegetables or sweets, an ironic gesture, vices to share.
Wishing Ganges to wash away sins, dear friend, it's not so,
True liberation lies in living, feeling nature's every glow.
I saw life in death, and realised our transient way,
True beauty lies in living, feeling every breath's display.
Our body is a temple of beats and breaths, rhythming to life's muse,
Death liberates the breath, caught in life's cage, to eternity.

Oceanic

Life is an ocean,
Wide, deep, and free,
Tides that rise and fall,
Tossing choices many.
Swim through torrents to soft sand,
Greeting the sea, with moments grand,
Enjoy those tiny peppers and moments of glee,

For Life is an ocean, Wide, deep, and free.
No tides, no glory,
En route, a happy journey!

Unbridled Inner Child

The Little girl inside me...
I see red, she sees blue,
I see challenge, she sees a clue.
The problem is old, the approach is new...
I see darkness, she sees stars,
I see rain, she sees a rainbow afar.
When life throws a curveball,
She's strong, sensible, and bold.
The Little girl inside me...
Sees everything from a unique perspective view,
A beacon of hope, a heart that's true,
A reminder to see the world anew.

Eternity is Now

Life takes place in this moment
The past-future subsists
in imagination
Let the twinkling seconds blink enjoyment..
Life is now

today's celebration!

Soulful Silence

Soulful silence, amidst the din,
Flashy distractions, empty diversions within,
Fleeting disquiets, that troubled mind,
Seek depth, and leave the chaos behind.
For life is within, a truth profound,
Inside out, where love and peace resound,
A world of wonder, where soul and heart
entwine,
Seek depth, and let the silence be your guide
divine.

Metamorphosis

Rebirth begins within, conceive life's depths,
and let meaning grow.
Recreate, evolve, ignite the spark,
Embracing flaws, be gentle with yourself, a
mother's loving heart.
Nourish your mind with pure intention,
Give birth to your renewed self, a radiant
transformation.
No one can save you, except yourself,
Accept, transform, and rise, a phoenix, reborn
and free.

Masquerade life

Life is a drama
We all play parts in long and shorts

The scenes differ the actors vary
A few draw close and some depart
The masquerade we wear to show the best of
ourselves to the world
contrast
Seldom I ponder
While I play the part, am I the actor or the
director of this work of art?
Am I wearing a mask or showing the world my
true heart?

Bougainvillea

Bougainvillaea, dancing free,
Hanging in lively spree,
Wild and untamed, a colourful sight,
Wearing pink, purple, blue, red, and more light.
So common, yet never a bore,
Light, quirky, and full of colour galore,
Glorious, yet unassuming and plain,
Inspiring us to cherish life's simple refrain,
Escaping the world's loud.

"Echoes of Uncertainty"

When asked if I'm depressed, I'm lost for
words,
Is anxiety and restlessness a sign, or just
blurred?
A void within, staring into oblivion's space,
Or numbing myself with comedy's fleeting
pace?
Or is it the thrill of horror movies, a shallow
escape?
I'm unsure if I'm depressed, but one thing's in
place,
A hollow pain in my chest, a constant ache,
No matter who I share it with, it never fades
away.

A Humble Stance

Nature heals itself, I'm not its saviour,
Seeds fall, and trees grow, in their own favour.
I'm not here to save the waters or mountains
high,
But to appreciate God's gifts, and ask not why.
Let me live life fully, with gratitude and care,
Recognising my role in preserving the earth we
share.
I'll use resources wisely, and tread with gentle
feet,
Grateful for life's blessings, and conserving for
what's to meet.
With a humble heart, I'll preserve what's divine,
What I cannot create, I must preserve in its
prime.
I'll protect and cherish, the beauty that's mine,
A responsible start, in harmony with nature's
design.

"Union of Souls"

Men are from Mars, women from Venus, they
meet on Earth to blend,
In a beautiful union, that will forever transcend.
Marriage, a sacred bond, two hearts, one soul,
Two brains, one mind, in perfect control.
Though formed between two, like proton and
neutron entwined,
They unite to become one atom, a love divine.
With vows and promises, mere words that bind,
Actions speak louder, to forever be aligned.
Not the threads or rings that hold, but the feeling
that grows,
A partner in crime, that gives you wings to soar
and glow.

Marriage, nature's gift to mankind, a treasure
rare,
Rituals may vary, but the bond that's formed is
beyond compare.
To unite in love, a bond that's strong and true,
Death cannot part, for you are one in heart and
mind, forever anew.
Like lyrics and music, making a perfect song,
Marriage is the culmination, of two opposite
units, bound to
harmonise, all day long.
In this beautiful dance, of love and life,
Two souls become one, in a union that's rife.

"Beat of Bliss"

I'm lost in music, a world of beats and rhymes,
From Carnatic to Vedic chants, my spirit aligns.
MSS's soothing melodies to Scorpions' rockin'
vibe,
Def Leopard, Sting, Metallica, Floyd, and
Linkin Park, my soul
thrives.
Some tunes give me chills, others set me free,
Instrumentals by Rahman, songs of SPB, KK,
and Karthik, a
symphony.
Their voices, a sweet escape, lyrics dipped in
sugar and love,
Kishore Da, my classic favourite, happy or sad,
sent from above.
My mom's a fan of Lata Mangeshkar, a legend
of old,
Her melodies still echo, stories untold.
I'm a hardcore fan of lyrics, but beats and
rhythm steal my heart,

My mind hums in loops, a melodic work of art.
In music's embrace, I find my peaceful place,
A world without it, would leave an empty space.
The rhythm of life, that beats in every part,
Music is my solace, forever in my heart.

"Empowered Feminity"

Women, a rare and precious breed,
Shining through tears, yet growing stronger still.
Laughing to ease worries, yet anxious every day,
Thriving to please others, sacrificing self-care
along the way.
We organise chaos, create order with ease,
Yet ponder daily, unsure of
"what to wear" with expertise.
Multitasking superpowers, we dedicate with
might,
Love, life, and family, our focus, day and night.
All we ask for is respect and trust,
But the world fails us, leaving us to rust.
A world without us would be dull and grey,

Flabbergasted, a world that's lost its way.
Women aren't showcase pieces of art, but
colours that make life bright,
Not burdens to carry, but shoulders that support
with all our might.
We don't need one day dedicated to celebrate
our existence,
We're queens, warriors, born to rule with
persistence.
We wear armour, blazers of strength and might,
Our beauty shines, a craft that's a wondrous
sight.
Understand us, and you'll see our worth,
We're the heartbeat of the world, a precious
birth.

A lasting Legacy

A forest of friendship, strong and deep,
Rooted in love, forever to keep.

Trees of trust, with branches wide,
Shading my path, side by side.
Diamonds of devotion, precious and rare,
Treasured bonds, beyond compare.
Unwavering love, unbreakable spirit,
A gift of friendship, forever to merit.
Through life's journey, friends appear,
In every walk, they calm my fear.
Their love and support, a guiding light,
Illuminating darkness, making everything right.
This forest of friendship, a treasure to behold,
A testament to love, that never grows old.
I cherish each tree, each bond so strong,
A friendship like no other, where I belong.

Beneath the petals

Like a daffodil, I conceal my soul,
A beautiful enigma, with secrets untold,
My mind a labyrinth, mysterious and deep,
Where turbulent thoughts and emotions silently
creep.
My heart is a maelstrom, hysterical and wild,
A chaos of voices, like whispers in a shell,
Echoes that haunt me, a cacophony of fears,
That I dare not speak, lest they bring forth tears.
Like poison in the bulb of the daffodil's might,
My darkness lies hidden, a toxic, deadly sight,
I fear myself, the venom that I hold within,
A dangerous allure, like the flower's sweet,
deceptive skin.

So I shield my consciousness, like the daffodil's
layers strong,
With petals of protection, to keep my demons
long,
For in the depths of my mind, a storm rages on,
A turmoil of thoughts, that I cannot outrun.
So I'll hold them close, like the daffodil's golden
core,
And keep them hidden, forever in store.

Life's Upswing

Faith is the force that's beyond clout and genius.
Get your hopes up, have belief in yourself, be
your own inspiration.
Life is driven by twists and turns; after all the
drama, good things
return.
For there's no roadmap to life that doesn't
include lows and highs.
So, smile when you feel like sighing!
Let your mind and body endure the pain; don't
give up, try again.

The Winds of July

I stand on the high-floor balcony,
As July's winds rush in like a wave's mighty
gush,
Swaying me gently, yet firmly, like a lover's
caress,
Playing wisely with my hair, a soothing
tenderness.
Bare feet on the floor, I feel the warm, cold chill,
As the wind whispers secrets, my soul starts to
fill,
Misting the dryness, cleansing my body and
mind,
Like tears to the soul, the wind's balm, I am
aligned.

In this moment, I ponder, if seasons weren't
designed,
How would our lives be, untwined from
experiences divine?
Would we know the beauty of growth, the pain
of decay?

Or would our stories be dull, without the winds
of change to sway?
You're so kind, thanks, my heart, every time,
The winds of July, your kindness echoes, a
gentle breeze
That soothes my heart, and brings me to my
knees
In gratitude, I feel my soul take flight.

"The Unseen Essential"

A flower's essence, distilled in amber's warm light,
Unfurls its mystique, in whispers through the night.
Ethereal and light, like a sylph's gentle touch,
A refined fragrance reveals a person's inner clutch.
Like a calligrapher's art or a poet's subtle flame,
A fragrance tells a tale of the heart's deepest name.
A good fragrance signifies a persona that's true,
A nuanced language, speaking volumes, in all you do.

"Thou Art That "

I am born, and told what's good, bad, easy, and
bold
Made to realise truth lies beyond what's been
told
Advised to pray to God until I grow old
Told that red, purple, blue, and black are colours,
but white is pure
gold
Explained why metals play a vital role
And I should aim for silver or gold
Sent to school to study and know
The science of tomorrow, from history's age-old
glow

But one fine day, I ask myself consciously
'Who am I?' Am I the opinions of others'
perception?
Or am I my own imagination?

Am I what's painted by an artist, or am I the
artisan?
Am I the body I love, or the mind within?
Or am I part of a whole system, a society from
all it began?
Am I part of the earth, soil, or trees around?
Or am I part of the stars and constellation?
What am I, or who am I? Is it a thin line of solid
complacency?
Or am I what my Guru tells, 'Tat Tvam Asi'?

"Vivid Voices"

Why should birds of the same feather flock
together?
If we all share the same opinions, where's the
newness to discover?
Singing the same repetitive tune isn't music to
our ears,
For a mature mind knows that opinions can vary,
and that's okay, my
dear.
We can agree to disagree, and still find common
ground,
For an open mind is all we need to turn
differences around.

We can be different and unique at the same time,
Making room for fresh ideas from every mind.
Don't be bound by limitations; life is vast and
wide,
Unwind and embrace the beauty of diverse
perspectives inside.

"Filtered Chronicles"

My roots run deep, sown in the southern ground
Born green, roasted to perfection, brown all
around
I'm enigmatically fresh and divine, setting souls
free

Liberating all with my aroma, reinvigorating you
and me
I'm bittersweet and coarse, yet low in calories
too
Even with whole milk and sucrose, my goodness
shines through
A culinary art, performed only by the chef pros
A few know the secret to pouring the perfect
decoction, don't you
know

I stand strong and bold, amongst all coffees worldwide
Filter coffee is my name, latte and cappuccino can't step inside
I'm good for heart and soul, in every season's tale
Rainy or shiny, I add taste and life to everything that prevails
I'm the almighty filter coffee, your old and trusted friend
Together forever, till the very end!

"Sky Vagabond "

Grateful for this life, I gaze beyond
If I could plan my next, I'd say I'm done
Pondering and wandering, lost in societal style
I yearn to soar like an astronaut, in the dark
sky's smile
As much as I love Earth, I want to travel far
Beyond this hive, to the cosmos, near and far
No more living to fulfil,l home loans and credit
card EMIs
I want to relish life, like a hippie in the cosmic
breeze
Place me on Mars, Venus, Pluto, Jupiter, or
Planet X

I'm okay with that, up there I'll find my next
flex
I want to wander, like a fairy in the night
With wings and pixie dust, sparkling with
delight
In the luminous moonshine, I'll find my way
A cosmic vagabond, in the stars, I'll play.

Binary consequences

Karma's binary code, a simple score
Good deeds yield zero, bad deeds one more
Tally rises with each wrong move
Clear your slate with a gentle groove
Choose right, in karma's binary move.

Gratitude & Echoes

With this verse, my naive beginning comes full
circle,
A 50-poem journey I never thought I'd unfurl.
Thanks to the universe's gentle nudge, I've
found my voice,
Pushing past limits, I've made my heart and soul
rejoice.
I hope these words have resonated with you, at
least once,
Thank you for reading; I look forward to your
thoughts, when our
paths cross again.
As Rumi's wisdom echoes, 'What you seek is
seeking you,'
I'm gratcful these words found me, and this
book came to be, for me
and for you.